Muslim Festival Tales

written by
Kerena Marchant

illustrated by
Tina Barber

HODDER
Wayland
An imprint of Hodder Children's Books

Festival Tales

Christian Festival Tales • Hindu Festival Tales
Jewish Festival Tales • Muslim Festival Tales

© 2000 White-Thomson Publishing Ltd

Produced for Hodder Wayland by
White-Thomson Publishing Ltd
2/3 St Andrew's Place
Lewes BN7 1UP

Series Concept: Saviour Pirotta/Philippa Smith/Polly Goodman
Editor: Margot Richardson
Designer: Jane Hawkins
Music Score: John Nicholson

'Beloved Messenger of Allah' © 1996 Ayesha bint Mahmood, published by
The Islamic Foundation in *Rays of Truth, Poems on Islam*.
'Eider Chand' © Oxford University Press 1986. Reproduced by permission. Licence no 05275.

Published in Great Britain by Hodder Wayland, an imprint of Hodder Children's Books
First published in paperback 2001
The right of Kerena Marchant to be identified as the author and Tina Barber as the illustrator
of this Work has been asserted by them in accordance with the Copyright, Designs and Patents Act 1988.

A catalogue record for this book is available from the British Library.

ISBN 0 7502 32811

Printed and bound in Italy by Eurografica Spa, Vicenza, Italy

Hodder Children's Books
A division of Hodder Headline Limited
338 Euston Road, London NW1 3BH

Please note that in respect to Muslim beliefs the Arabic symbol ﷺ,
which stands for *sallallahu alaihi wa sallam* (peace and blessings of Allah
upon him), appear after the names of prophets in this book.

Contents

Al Qaswa's Hijrah

The Hijrah was when the Prophet Muhammad ﷺ and his followers migrated from Makkah to Madinah. This story of the Hijrah is told from the perspective of al Qaswa, the Prophet Muhammad's ﷺ camel.

Night fell over the city of Makkah and all the houses became dark shadows. The only thing that stood out in the darkness was al Qaswa, the white camel. Al Qaswa regarded herself as the luckiest camel in Makkah, not because she was the most beautiful or the fastest, but because she was owned by the Prophet Muhammad ﷺ. The Prophet ﷺ loved animals and always treated her kindly, giving her plenty of water to drink and food to eat. When it was hot, he would make sure she kept cool in the shade.

Al Qaswa loved her kind master but many people in Makkah did not. This was because they believed that there were many gods, and they made lots of money selling statues of the gods and by selling animals for sacrifice to the gods. Muhammad ﷺ taught that there was only one God, Allah, and that idol worship and animal sacrifice was wrong. Many realised that Muhammad ﷺ was right and stopped buying statues and animals for sacrifice. Muhammad ﷺ was bad for business and his enemies wanted him killed.

Suddenly, al Qaswa heard footsteps. She saw a shadowy group of men creep across the courtyard to her master's window. 'We must kill him tonight,' they whispered. Al Qaswa feared for her master's safety but soon the men crept away and she thought the danger had passed.

At dawn, al Qaswa heard footsteps again. The men had returned, and she feared that her master would die! Suddenly, the door burst open and the Prophet's ﷺ cousin, Ali, stood there. 'You will not find Muhammad ﷺ!' he cried. 'He has escaped!' The assassins ran off to find the Prophet ﷺ and to kill him.

Al Qaswa wished she could bear her master away to safety. She was the fastest camel and no one would catch them, but all she could do was wait and hope that her master had escaped.

Three days and nights passed. Al Qaswa was treated well while a friend of her master's looked after her. She learnt that her master was still alive, but a reward of a hundred camels had been offered to whoever could find him and kill him.

The next night, al Qaswa and another camel were woken up and led out of the courtyard, down the back streets and out of the city of Makkah. Soon, they came to a cave. Inside the cave, she saw her beloved master alive and well with his friend, Abu Bakar. 'To the city of Madinah!' Abu Bakar cried.

They did not travel to Madinah the usual way in case someone saw them, but made a detour across the mountains and desert. Days and nights passed and they had no food or drink. One night, they met some merchants who sold them some clean white clothes, food and water.

Soon after, they reached the city of Madinah. As soon as the people of Madinah saw the Prophet ﷺ, they rushed out to greet him. Children took al Qaswa by the reins and stroked her nose.

Al Qaswa proudly led the procession through the streets of the city. 'Come and live in my house!' the people begged the Prophet ﷺ as he passed by. Al Qaswa wondered which house her master would choose to live in.

Suddenly, the Prophet ﷺ halted and dismounted to pray. After his prayer, he mounted al Qaswa again and whispered to her. She raised her proud head and her master let go of her reins. Slowly she walked, step by step. The silent crowd followed behind, step by step. No reins guided her: she was guided by Allah. Eventually she felt told to stop and she knelt down beside a barn. Everybody cheered and a cry went up, 'Here shall the Prophet ﷺ build his mosque and his home, and with these people shall he stay!'

Beloved Messenger of Allah

Meelad-ul-Nabal is a celebration of the birth of the Prophet Muhammad ﷺ when Muslims tell stories, poems or sing songs about the Prophet ﷺ. It is also a time when Muslims think about how they can best follow his example.

Although I never saw your face
So beautiful, bestowed with grace
My heart doth yearn to be like you
In thoughts and hopes and actions too
You loved the children and the old
And gave your heart to every soul
You nursed the sick and served the poor
And fed the hungry at your door
You loved the creatures – tame and wild
And comforted the orphan child
You bid men peace, cared for the youth,
God's Messenger in truth!

King Hakim's Garden

Two weeks before the fast of Ramadan, at Laylat-ul-Barh, Muslims prepare themselves for the fast by remembering their sins and asking Allah to forgive them. This is a story that would be told around this time.

Cast of Characters

King Hakim
The king's vizier
The royal courtiers
The royal gardeners

Soldiers
The widow
The qadi, a judge
A donkey

Scene 1: The king's garden and the widow's garden

The stage is divided in half by a fence. To the right is the king's garden with trees, grass, roses and a royal seat overlooking the widow's garden. To the left is the widow's garden which is full of vegetables: courgettes, peppers, aubergines, carrots, onions, pumpkins and pomegranate trees. The widow is busy watering and weeding her garden.

The king, his vizier and his courtiers enter. The king sits on his seat.

Courtier 1: Your majesty has the most beautiful garden in the kingdom.

Courtier 2: Your roses, their scent…! Beautiful!

Courtier 3: Everybody in the kingdom envies your garden.

Vizier: Your majesty, it is such a shame that when you sit in your garden you have to look at that… um… vegetable garden. It does spoil your view.

The courtiers nod in agreement.

King Hakim: You are right! I will buy that garden.

Courtier 1: You must do that your majesty!

Courtier 2: Think what you could do with it.

Courtier 3: You could build a fountain and a pond!

Courtier 1: Or a summer house.

King Hakim (To the vizier): Give the woman two bags of gold for her garden.

The vizier goes to the fence and summons the widow. The king and his courtiers watch with interest.

11

Vizier: Woman, come here!

The widow obediently comes over, wiping her muddy hands. She kneels but the vizier indicates for her to stand.

Vizier: Woman, the king will buy your garden! Take these two bags of gold and be gone!
Widow: This is my garden. I will not sell it! Without this garden, I cannot grow vegetables to eat and sell.
Vizier: The king orders you to sell your garden! You must obey him!

The courtiers nod in agreement.

Widow: The king orders me to die. If I have no garden, I have no food. I will have nothing to sell or eat. I will starve to death.
Vizier: You will have this gold.
Widow: Gold does not last long.

The vizier walks back to consult with the king.

Vizier: Your majesty, the woman won't sell.

King: Give her whatever she wants! A hundred bags of gold. Bring me my gold!

The soldiers walk on carrying a heavy chest of gold.

Vizier: Woman, the king has been generous. He will give you as much gold as you want for your garden.
Widow: I will not sell my garden for all the gold in the kingdom. Allah has given me this garden to look after and I will not sell it!

The vizier goes back to consult with the king.

Vizier: Your majesty, the woman still will not sell.
King: Then take the garden by force! I am the king. I will be obeyed!

The soldiers take down the fence. The king and his courtiers watch with interest.

Widow: Allah, help me! How can I now earn money? How can I eat?

The gardeners come in and pull up the vegetables, watched by the royal party.

Widow: I must find the qadi quickly! He is wise. He will know what to do!

She leaves and quickly returns with the qadi. The gardeners are carrying away the vegetables.

Widow: See for yourself! My garden has been taken.

Vizier: Qadi, the woman refused money so we had to take the garden by force. If the king wants the garden, he must have it.

King: Good day, Qadi. The blessings of Allah be upon you. Do you like my new garden? Do you think I should build a fountain or a summer house here?

Qadi: Your majesty, courtiers, gardeners, soldiers, stop your work! We must all meet here tomorrow to decide what must be done with this garden. The widow must be here too.

King: So you're not sure if a fountain or a summer-house would be best?

Qadi: I will think about it and meet you tomorrow.

Vizier: The qadi is wise, your majesty. He will give you good advice.

King: We shall all meet here tomorrow.

Vizier: These are the king's orders!

The king leaves followed by the vizier, his courtiers, the soldiers and the gardeners. The widow takes a last look at her garden and leaves crying. The qadi is alone.

Qadi: What am I to do? The king has done wrong, but how can I tell the king that? Oh dear! I must think of something. Allah, help me!

He walks off, thinking.

Scene 2: It is the next day.

Soldier: I call upon you to assemble. The king has ordered the qadi to decide what must be done with the garden.

The qadi arrives in the king's part of the garden with a donkey and some sacks. The widow arrives and waits in her garden, watching. The widow and the qadi kneel. The king, vizier, courtiers and gardeners arrive. The king indicates that the qadi and the widow should stand.

King: Good day, Qadi. The blessings of Allah be upon you today.
Qadi: May Allah bless you and give you wisdom. I hope you don't mind me bringing my donkey into your garden?

King: Not at all. Tell me, what should I build in my new garden: a fountain or a summer house?

Qadi: I have the answer, but first can I ask a favour, your majesty?

King: Ask and it shall be granted.

Qadi: Can I have some sacks of soil from your majesty's garden for my garden?

King: Some soil? Soil! Of, of… course. Gardeners, fill the qadi's sacks!

The gardeners go to the widow's garden to dig up the soil. The widow is horrified and falls to her knees praying.

Qadi: (pointing at the king's part of the garden): I'd like the soil from there, please.

King: (not happy): Of course. Do as the qadi wishes.

The gardeners dig up the soil and put it into sacks. The soldiers load the sacks on to the donkey. The donkey brays and shows the weight of the sacks. The widow cries and prays. The king and his court watch in bewilderment and horror as the garden is dug up. Finally, the donkey can carry no more sacks and brays mournfully.

Vizier: Qadi, your donkey can take no more soil. You have enough!

Qadi: I want more!

King: Qadi, you are wise. Tell me why you want more soil than you can carry away?

Qadi: Your majesty, you yourself have done that when you took the widow's garden from her.

King: I'm not quite with you, Qadi.

Qadi: The soil is like our sins. When we die, we will all face Allah on the day of judgement carrying all our sins with us. Allah will see all our sins and judge us. Those of us with sins will not enter Paradise.

Everybody: Allah be merciful to us!

Qadi: Your majesty, if you take the widow's garden you will have more sins than you can carry on the day of judgement. You will be like that donkey with the soil. Do you expect Allah to forgive all those sins and let you enter Paradise?

The king kneels.

King: May Allah forgive me! Qadi, you are right. If I take the widow's garden, I will have more sins than I can carry on the day of judgement. Allah would show me no mercy.

Qadi: You must ask the widow's forgiveness and pay her back for all the vegetables you have dug up. Your gardeners must replant her garden.

King: I ask your forgiveness, good woman.

Widow: May Allah forgive you.

Qadi: May Allah have mercy on you on the day of judgement and let you see Paradise.

Everybody: May Allah show mercy.

King: Give the widow a chest of gold and replant her garden.

The soldiers leave and reappear with a chest of gold. The gardeners start to dig the garden and plant vegetables with the widow supervising. The king and his court leave, then the qadi and his donkey leave.

Stuffed Dates

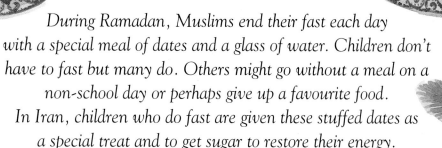

*During Ramadan, Muslims end their fast each day
with a special meal of dates and a glass of water. Children don't
have to fast but many do. Others might go without a meal on a
non-school day or perhaps give up a favourite food.
In Iran, children who do fast are given these stuffed dates as
a special treat and to get sugar to restore their energy.*

12 dates
(large dried dates such as
Medjool are the best)
50 g pistachio nuts (optional)

50 g sultanas   2 dstsp runny honey
25 g ground almonds   Few drops rose water

1 Cut a hole along the dates and carefully take out
   the stones.
2 Mix the pistachio nuts and sultanas in a bowl.
3 Add the ground almonds and mix.
4 Add the honey and the rose water and mix all
   the ingredients well.
5 Put a teaspoon of the mixture into each date.

Eider Chand

This is a song from Bengal. Eider Chand means Id Moon in Bengali.
Throughout the world, everybody looks out for the new moon which will
mean that Ramadan has ended and the festivities of Id-ul-Fitr can begin after
prayers. After the fast, everybody is closer to Allah and each other.
This is what is celebrated at Id-ul-Fitr.

I can see the Eid moon shin-ing high, – –

Show me where it shines up in the sky. – –

From to-day we will sing and play, we will all be friends to-geth-er.

From to-day we will sing and play, we will all be friends to-geth-er.

I can see the Eid moon shin-ing high, – –

Show me where it shines up in the sky. –

You can do a dance to this song.
Join hands in a circle.
1 When you sing the first line, take seven steps to the left and stop.
2 During the singing of line 2, take seven steps to the right and stop.
3 During line 3, clap your hands, skip into the middle of the circle and out.
4 During line 4, skip round with a partner.
5 For line 5, take seven steps to the left.
6 For line 6, take seven steps to the right, stop and clap.

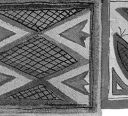

Ali's Hajj

*The Prophet Muhammad ﷺ commanded every Muslim who could afford it
to go on Hajj (pilgrimage) to Makkah at least once in their lifetime.
This pilgrimage is undertaken during the month of the Hajj.
Many Muslims will spend a lifetime saving for this.*

There was a poor man called Ali. All his life he had carefully saved up money so that he could go on Hajj, as ordered in the Qur'an. Year after year he saved until he was an old man. One day, he had saved enough money and he could go on Hajj to Makkah that year.

The night before he was to go on Hajj, Ali laid out the special clothes that he would wear on Hajj: two unsewn sheets of white cloth. His life's dream had come true! He was going to go on Hajj before he died.

He decided to go and say goodbye to his neighbour before he set off. When he arrived at his neighbour's house, he knocked on the door but nobody answered. Eventually, he opened the door and saw his neighbour on his bed, sick and close to death. Ali knew that if his friend had enough money for a doctor he would get better, but his friend was poor and had no money. Ali sadly bid him farewell and went home to prepare for his Hajj.

All night, Ali couldn't sleep. His friend would die because he had no money for a doctor. Ali had the money for a doctor but it was his Hajj money. He knew he would die before he could save that money again. What should he do? Go on Hajj or save his friend?

At dawn, he prayed and made his decision. He took his money to the doctor and asked him to cure his friend. He then sadly watched the people in his village leaving on Hajj.

Eventually, Ali's friend got better. The people who had gone on Hajj returned. They raced up to Ali and asked him how he had got home from the Hajj at Makkah so quickly and why he didn't travel with them. 'I didn't go on Hajj,' Ali replied. 'You did!' they chorused. 'We saw you circle the Ka'bah, and on the plain of Arafat with all the other pilgrims in your white clothes!'

Giving the money to his sick friend was seen by Allah as Ali's Hajj, and so he had gone on Hajj in spirit.

The Sacrifice of Isma'il ﷺ

Id-ul-Adha is the feast of the sacrifice. This festival was introduced by the Prophet Muhammad ﷺ and remembers the time when Ibrahim ﷺ showed his obedience to Allah by obeying Allah's command to sacrifice his son, Isma'il ﷺ.

There was once a Muslim Prophet called Ibrahim ﷺ. He lived many years after Adam ﷺ, the first man, had built the Ka'bah in Makkah as a place of prayer to the One God, and long before the Prophet Muhammad ﷺ taught people about the One God.

Ibrahim ﷺ lived at a time when people no longer worshipped the One God as their ancestor Adam ﷺ had done, but worshipped a number of different gods who did not exist. They prayed and bowed to statues of these gods, believing that these empty actions proved that they lived good lives. They also sacrificed animals to the statues, thinking that the animals' deaths would make amends for their wrong-doings – but they made no effort to live better lives.

Ibrahim ﷺ was different. He believed in the One God and was known as 'the friend of God'. So great was Ibrahim's ﷺ love for Allah, and so obedient was he to Allah's commands, that he vowed to sacrifice everything he had to Allah if he was ever asked: his house, his land, his wealth – and even his own life.

Ibrahim ﷺ had two wives: Sarah, and an Egyptian wife called Hagar. For many years, Ibrahim ﷺ was childless and he was an old man when Hagar finally gave birth to a son, Isma'il ﷺ. Isma'il ﷺ was the most precious thing to Ibrahim ﷺ.

One night, Allah spoke to Ibrahim ﷺ in a dream and commanded him to sacrifice his beloved son, Isma'il ﷺ. Ibrahim ﷺ loved his son and was grief stricken at the thought of sacrificing him, but he knew he had to obey Allah's command.

Satan decided to test Ibrahim's ﷺ love and obedience to Allah. He tried to persuade Ibrahim ﷺ that his dream was not a message from Allah. Ibrahim ﷺ knew his dream to be a message from Allah and sent Satan away.

Next, Satan visited Hagar, Isma'il's ﷺ mother, and tried to persuade her to try to save her son. Hagar knew that her husband's dream was a message from Allah and sent Satan away.

Finally, Satan tried to persuade Isma'il ﷺ to try to save his own life. Isma'il ﷺ knew that his sacrifice was the will of Allah and picked up a stone to drive Satan away. Ibrahim ﷺ and Hagar also drove off Satan with stones.

Ibrahim ﷺ then asked his son if he wanted to go through with the sacrifice. 'Do as Allah commands you,' Isma'il ﷺ replied.

Both father ﷺ and son ﷺ prepared to carry out Allah's command. For Ibrahim ﷺ this meant killing his beloved son and for Isma'il ﷺ it meant death. Isma'il ﷺ lay face downwards, and Ibrahim ﷺ lifted his knife to sacrifice his son.

But when the knife fell, Allah put a ram in the place of Isma'il ﷺ, and Isma'il ﷺ was saved from death. Both Ibrahim ﷺ and Isma'il ﷺ had done what Allah had asked in the dream. They proved that their faith and obedience to Allah came first, even if it meant Ibrahim ﷺ sacrificing his son and Isma'il ﷺ giving up his own life.

Allah rewarded Ibrahim ﷺ for his obedience. Sarah, Ibrahim's ﷺ other wife, gave birth to a son called Isaac. The two sons of Ibrahim ﷺ became the fathers of the people who were the first to believe in the One God. Isma'il ﷺ was the father of the Muslim people, and Isaac was the father of the Jewish people.

Dhul-Hijjah

8th-10th – The Hajj
10-12th – Id-ul-Adha

Dhul-Qad'ah

Festival Information

The Muslim calendar is called the Hijrah. There are twelve months and each month lasts from one new moon to the next, so each month contains 29 or 30 days.

AL HIJRAH (THE MIGRATION)   The first day of the new year. Muslims date their calendar from the time of the Hijrah when the Prophet Muhammad ﷺ and his followers migrated from Makkah to Madinah.

MEELAD-UL-NABAL   celebrates the birth of the Prophet Muhammad ﷺ. Sunni and Shi'ah Muslims have different dates for this celebration – the 12th and 17th – so the week that lies between the two dates is a week of Islamic Unity.

WOMEN'S DAY   The birthday of the Prophet Muhammad's ﷺ daughter, Fatimah, is celebrated on the 20th day of the month of Jamada al-Thani. In Iran, this day is celebrated as women's or mothers' day.

LAYLAT-UL-ISRA (THE NIGHT JOURNEY) A commemoration of the night that the Angel Jibril took the Prophet Muhammad ﷺ to heaven. There Muhammad ﷺ toured the seven heavens and negotiated with God over how many times a day Muslims should pray.

LAYLAT-UL-BARH   This is the night of forgiveness which comes two weeks before the fast of Ramadan. Muslims prepare themselves spiritually for the fast by remembering their sins and asking God to forgive them. Muslims take sins seriously as they believe that on the day of judgement those who have sinned will not be allowed into Paradise.

RAMADAN   The holy month of Ramadan is when Muslims fast as ordered in the Qur'an. This is a time of spiritual celebration, as it is during this time that Muslims feel closer to God.

Laylat-ul-Qadr, the 23rd–27th night of Ramadan, is the Night of Power, the anniversary of the night that the Angel Jibril visited the Prophet Muhammad ﷺ in a cave on Mount Hira and revealed the Qur'an to him.

ID-UL-FITR   is the festival that celebrates the end of the Ramadan fast and was introduced by the Prophet Muhammad ﷺ. It is a festival that begins with prayer and charity at the mosque.

AL HAJJ   The Prophet Muhammad ﷺ commanded every Muslim who could afford it to go on Hajj (pilgrimage) to Makkah at least once in their lifetime. This pilgrimage is undertaken during the month of the Hajj. Muslims go on this pilgrimage to Makkah because the Ka'bah is there. This is the shrine that Adam ﷺ, the first man, built to honour Allah, which was later rebuilt by Ibrahim ﷺ. On Hajj, pilgrims remember events that took place in the lives of Ibrahim ﷺ, Hagar and Isma'il ﷺ.
The Plain of Arafat is a few kilometres from Makkah. It is where pilgrims gather to worship, pray and ask for forgiveness on the ninth day of the month of Dhul-Hijjah.

ID-UL-ADHA   (THE FEAST OF THE SACRIFICE) This festival comes at the end of the Hajj and was introduced by the Prophet Muhammad ﷺ. It remembers the time when Ibrahim ﷺ showed his obedience to God by obeying His command to sacrifice his son, Isma'il ﷺ, and how God showed His mercy by putting a ram in Isma'il's ﷺ place. It is a time when Muslims remember that they have to sacrifice everything for God and Islam. During this feast, everybody shares a traditional dish of lamb.

Glossary

Allah The Arabic name for God. Muslims believe that there is only one God, whom they call Allah.

Detour Travelling by a round-about way, usually to avoid something on the most direct way.

Hajj The Arabic word for pilgrimage. Muslims go on Hajj to Makkah during the month of the Hajj, Dhul-Hijjah.

Ibrahim One of Allah's Prophets. He is known to Christians and Jews as Abraham. His first son, Isma'il, was the father of the Muslims and his other son, Isaac, the father of the Jewish people.

Islam Means 'to submit' and is the name of the Muslim way of life. Muslims believe they must submit to the will of Allah in every part of life.

Jibril The angel who recited the Qur'an to Muhammad in the cave on Mount Hira and accompanied Muhammad on his journey into heaven. Christians call Jibril Gabriel.

Ka'bah A black, cube-shaped structure in the centre of the Grand Mosque in Makkah. Some Muslims believe that it was built by Adam, the first man, as a place of prayer to Allah.

Makkah A city in present-day Saudi Arabia. Only Muslims can visit this Holy city which houses the Ka'bah and was the birthplace of the Prophet Muhammad.

Madinah A city in present-day Saudi Arabia, where the Prophet Muhammad lived after his move from Makkah and is buried. Madinah is the second most sacred city in Islam, after Makkah.

Mosque A place where Muslims worship.

Muslim A follower of Islam. A Muslim believes that there is one God, Allah, and lives their life according to what Allah wants them to do, as written in the Qur'an.

Prophet A person chosen by God to instruct people as to the will of God. Some of the Muslim prophets are the same as the Jewish and Christian prophets. They include Jesus, and Muhammad who is the last of the prophets.

Qadi A judge, whose job was to settle disputes between people.

Qur'an The Muslim Holy book which was revealed to the Prophet Muhammad by the Angel Jibril.

Ram A male sheep.

Sacrifice Killing an animal or person, or giving something up, as proof of someone's obedience to God.

Vizier A king's most important advisor.

Worshippers People who give honour and respect to God, especially in a mosque, synagogue or church.

Jamada al-Awwal

Jamada al-Thani

20th – The birthday of the Prophet Muhammad's daughter, Fatimah.

Index

Resources

Books
Islamic Festivals, by Khadijah Knight (Heinemann, 1995)
My Muslim Faith, by Khadijah Knight (Evans Brothers, 1999)
Rays of Truth, Poems on Islam, by Ayesha bint Mahmood
(The Islamic Foundation, 1996)
Marvellous Stories from the Life of Muhammad ﷺ,
by Mardijah A. Tarantino (The Islamic Foundation, 1995)
Id-ul-fitr, by Kerena Marchant (Wayland 1995)

Web sites
http://www.islam.org
IslamiCity in Cyberspace. Attractive site that explains
about Islam, has a virtual mosque tour and a children's page:
http://www.islam.org/KidsCorner/Default.htm

Other media resources
BBC Education produces schools programmes, videos and
resource packs on different faiths, including *Pathways of Belief*.
BBC Information, PO Box 1116, Belfast BT2 7AJ
Tel: 08700 100 222
email: info@bbc.co.uk
www.bbc.co.uk/schools

Channel 4 produces schools programmes, videos and
resource packs on different faiths, including
'Animated World Faiths'.
PO Box 100, Warwick CV34 6TZ
Tel: 01926 436444
email: sales@schools.channel4.co.uk
www.channel4.com/schools

For further information, books and resources
The Islamic Foundation, Markfield Dawah Centre,
Ratby Lane, Markfield, Leicester LE67 9RN

The Muslim Educational Trust, 130 Stroud Green Road,
London N4 3RZ   Tel: 020 7272 8502

The Islamic Cultural Centre, 146 Park Road , London NW8
Tel: 020 7724 3363

The Commonwealth Institute Resource Centre
Kensington High Street, London W8 6NQ
Tel 020 7603 4535
http://www.commonwealth.org.uk